Showhouse Review

An Exposé of Interior Decorating Events

Tina Skinner

4880 Lower Valley Road, Atglen, Pennsylvania 19310

Showhouse Review

An Exposé of Interior Decorating Events

Cover Design by Bruce Waters / Cover image courtesy of Ruth Cook, Photography by Randall Perry
Type set in Monotype Corsiva/Caslon224 Bk BT
Printed in China

Schiffer Books are available at special discounts for bulk purchases for sales promotions or premiums. Special editions, including personalized covers, corporate imprints, and excerpts can be created in large quantities for special needs. For more information contact the publisher.

Published by Schiffer Publishing Ltd.
4880 Lower Valley Road
Atglen, PA 19310
Phone: (610) 593-1777; Fax: (610) 593-2002
E-mail: Info@schifferbooks.com

For the largest selection of fine reference books on this and related subjects, please visit our web site at
www.schifferbooks.com
We are always looking for people to write books on new and related subjects. If you have an idea for a book please contact us at the above address.

This book may be purchased from the publisher.
Include $3.95 for shipping.
Please try your bookstore first.
You may write for a free catalog.

In Europe, Schiffer books are distributed by
Bushwood Books
6 Marksbury Ave.
Kew Gardens
Surrey TW9 4JF England
Phone: 44 (0) 20 8392-8585; Fax: 44 (0) 20 8392-9876
E-mail: info@bushwoodbooks.co.uk
Website: www.bushwoodbooks.co.uk
Free postage in the U.K., Europe; air mail at cost.

Contents

Foyers &
Hallways

Kimura Design: Sandra Kimura
Bellarmine University Women's Council Designers' Show House 2004
Photography: Katie Woodring

Details Interiors

Bellarmine University Women's Council Designers' Show House 2005
Designers: Lesa Buckley, Carrie Harvey, Cindy Alberding-Druin
Photography: Katie Woodring

Lewis Interiors

Bellarmine University Women's Council Designers' Show House 2005
Designer: Beth C. Lewis, ASID
Photography: Katie Woodring

Remarkable Interiors

Bellarmine University Women's Council Designers' Show House 2006
Designers: Lynnda-Marie Davis, Rebecca Schneider, & Sherry "O" Oexman

Tassels
Bellarmine University Women's Council Designers' Showhouse 2006
Designers: Kevin Coleman, Marsha Riggle & Jason Beck
Photography: Donna Borden

Experience and Creative Design, Ltd.

Vanguard/Albany Symphony Designers' Showhouse 2005
Designers: Rudy Grant & David Siders
Photography: Randall Perry

Norwalk – The Furniture Idea

Mid-Atlantic Center for the Arts, Cape May 2006 Designer Showhouse
Designer: Mark Little
Photography: John Armich

Whitney Design Associates

Boys' and Girls' Club 2007
ASID Designer Showhouse
Designer: Tom Stanley, ASID
Photography: Mark Borosch

Studies &
Libraries

Denise Maurer Interiors
Vanguard/Albany Symphony Decorators' Showhouse 2005
Decorative Painting: Elizabeth Rae Art Studios, Betsy Rae Mattice
Photography: Randall Perry

Classic Interiors
Vanguard/Albany Symphony Decorators' Showhouse 2007
Designer: Lynn Ricci and Jessica Hartgraves
Photography: Randall Perry

Window Wear, Etc.

Vanguard/Albany Symphony Decorators' Showhouse 2006
Designer: Terry L. Kral, ASID
Photography: Randall Perry

Kenneth/Davis, Inc. Architecture Interior Design

Mansion in May 2006
Designer: Davis F. Tamburin, R.A.
Photography: Peter Rymwid

Baker-Wooley Interiors

Vanguard/Albany Symphony Decorators' Showhouse 2005
Designer: James Brookens
Decorative Artist: Nora Lagan
Photography: Randall Perry

Whitney Stewart Interior Design

2003 Designer's Showcase at the Center for Family Development in Bethesda, Maryland
Photography: Whitney Stewart

Your Home

Bellarmine University Women's Council Designers' Show House 2005
Designers: Phillip Wheeler, Jason Beck & Stephen Lindsey
Photography: Katie Woodring

Interiors by Herbal Accents

Bellarmine University Women's Council Designers' Show House 2004
Designers: Julie Lund and Jason Jennings
Photography: Katie Woodring

Bittners, LLC

Bellarmine University Women's Council Designers' Show House 2004
Designer: Amy Frankenberger Cimba, CID
Photography: Katie Woodring

Whitney Stewart Interior Design

CEO Design House Spring 2005
Designer: Whitney Stewart
Photography: The Washington Design Center

Renaissance, Inc. Interior Design
Bellarmine University Women's Council Designers' Showhouse 2006
Designers: Kelli L. Milligan & Deborrah M. Tatum
Photography: Donna Borden

Dragonfly Interiors, LLC

Mid-Atlantic Center for the Arts, Cape May 2006 Designer Showhouse
Designer: Jan Schmidt
Photography: John Armich

Milieu Design Group
Christmas House 2006
Designer: Margaret Norcott
Photography: Burt Welleford

Drake Design Associates
Kips Bay Showhouse 2007
Designer: Jamie Drake
Photography: Nick Johnson

Nathan Egan Interiors
Kips Bay Showhouse 2007
Designer: Nathan Egan
Photography: Nick Johnson

CMH Design
Vanguard/Albany Symphony Decorators' Showhouse 2006
Designer: Cheryl M. Haitsch
Photography: Randall Perry

Living
Rooms

The Noel Jeffery Design Group, Inc.

Kips Bay Showhouse 2007
Designer: Noel Jeffery
Photography by Nick Johnson

The Noel Jeffery Design Group, Inc.
Kips Bay Showhouse 2007
Designer: Noel Jeffery
Photography by Nick Johnson

Christopher Gaona, Inc.
Beverly Hills Garden & Design Showcase 2006
Designer: Christopher Gaona Allied ASID

Tassels

Bellarmine University Women's Council Designers' Show House 2004
Designers: Marsha Riggle, Kevin Coleman, & Lisa Bizzell
Photography: Katie Woodring

Cherry House Furniture Galleries

Bellarmine University Women's Council Designers' Show House 2005
Designer: Laura Pennington
Photography: Katie Woodring

Thomasville Home Furnishings

Vanguard/Albany Symphony Decorators' Showhouse 2006
Designer: Jeffery Ture
Photography: Randall Perry

Hudson River Fine Interiors
Vanguard/Albany Symphony Decorators' Showhouse 2005
Designer: Michael J.M. Patterson
Wall Glaze: Mary Beth Johnson, A.R.T.
Photography: Randall Perry

Hudson River Fine Interiors
Vanguard/Albany Symphony Decorators' Showhouse 2005
Designer: Michael J. M. Patterson
Photography: Randall Perry

Sutton's Marketplace
Vanguard/Albany Symphony Decorators' Showhouse 2007
Designer: Edie Neely
Photography: Randall Perry

Hubbuch & Company

Bellarmine University Women's Council Designers' Showhouse 2006
Designers: Stephanie Wilson & Tommy Kute, Assoc. AIA
Photography: Donna Borden

Eve Robinson Assoc., Inc.
Kips Bay Show House, New York 2007
Designer: Eve Robinson ASID
Photographer: Phillip Ennis

Pedlar's Village Interior Design
Boys' and Girls' Club 2007 ASID Designer Showhouse
Designer: Gary Ficht, ASID
Photography: Mark Borosch

Eve Robinson Assoc., Inc.
Kips Bay Showhouse 2007
Designer: Eve Robinson
Photography: Nick Johnson

Eric Schmidt Interiors

Society of the Arts Designer's Showhouse, Allentown, PA 2006
Designer: Eric Schmidt ASID
Photography: Peter Gourniak, & Andrea Mittica

Healing Barsanti, Inc.
Kips Bay Showhouse 2007
Designers: Patricia Healing & Daniel Barsanti
Photography: Nick Johnson

Stephen Miller Seigel Architects
Kips Bay Showhouse 2007
Designer: Steven Miller Seigel
Photography: Nick Johnson

Magnolia Interiors

Mid-Atlantic Center for the Arts, Cape May 2006 Designer Showhouse
Designer: Susan Conroy
Photography: John Armich

Hubbuch & Co.
Bellarmine University Women's Council Designers' Show House 2006
Designers: Stephanie Wilson & Tommy Kute
Photography: John Paul

Mario Buatta, Inc.
Kips Bay Showhouse 2007
Designer: Mario Buatta
Photography: Nick Johnson

Lancaster Humma White Studio

Boys and Girls Club 2006 ASID Designer Showhouse
Designers: Bonnie Lancaster ASID & Keffie Lancaster
Photography: Keffie Lancaster

J. Hirsch Interior Design
Christmas House, 2006
Designer: Janie Hirsch, ASID, IFDA
Photography: Robert Thien, Inc.

Wendy Holden & Associates
Mid-Atlantic Center for the Arts, Cape May 2006 Designer Showhouse
Designer: Wendy Holden
Photography: John Armich

Cherry House, Inc.
Bellarmine University Women's Council
Designers' Show House 2006
Designer: Jackie Iler
Photography: Donna Borden

Carl Harz Furniture

Mid-Atlantic Center for the Arts, Cape May 2006 Designer Showhouse
Designer: Terri Bell
Photography: John Armich

Pineapple House Interior Design, Inc.
Atlanta Symphony Associates Decorators' Show House and Garden 2007
Photography: Chris Little Photography

Ethan Allen Home Interiors
Bellarmine University Women's Council Designers' Show House 2005
Designers: Patsy Grudzielanek & Rose Sweet-Pinard
Photography: Katie Woodring

Sitting, Gathering, & Keeping

Gryphon Interiors, Inc.

Bellarmine University Women's Council Designers' Show House 2006
Designer: David F. Arnold, CID
Photography: Donna Borden

Robb & Stucky Design

Boys' and Girls' Club 2007 ASID Designer Showhouse
Designer: Jeff Hart, ASID
Photography: Mark Borosch

Hudson River Fine Interiors

Vanguard/Albany Symphony Decorators' Showhouse 2007
Designer: Michel J.M. Patterson
Decorative Painter: Mary Beth Johnson, A.R.T.
Custom Floor: Kristin Holmes-Linder of khl Studio
Photography: Randall Perry

Gary Stewart Interiors

Bellarmine University Women's Council Designers' Show House 2005
Designer: Gary Stewart
Photography: Katie Woodring

The Replogle House Interiors
The Harrisburg Symphony Showhouse 2006
Designer: Diane Replogle ASID

J. Hirsch Interior Design

Decorator Show House & Gardens, Atlanta, Georgia 2007
Designer: Janie Hirsch, ASID, IFDA
Photography: Lauren Rubenstein

Kelley Interior Designs

National Symphony Orchestra Show House, Potomac, Maryland 2006
Designer: Kelley Proxmire
Photography: Angie Seckinger

Eric Schmidt Interiors

The Architectural Digest Home Design Show, New York 2004
Designer: Eric Schmidt ASID
Photography: James Dean

Michael Donnelly Interiors

Junior League of Buffalo Decorators' Show House 2007

Designers: Michael Donnelly & Tony Rogers

Photography: © 2007 Michael Mandolfo

Quaker Country Home
Junior League of Buffalo Decorators' Show House 2007
Designer: Pamela Witte
Photography: © 2007 Michael Mandolfo

La Bella Casa Designs, LLC

Mid-Atlantic Center for the Arts, Cape May 2006 Designer Showhouse
Designer: Lucille Mauriello
Photography: John Armich

Whitney Stewart Interior Design

International Influences, Spring 2000 Design House
Designer: Whitney Stewart
Photography: Walter Smalling, Jr.

Sally Trout Interiors

Boys' and Girls' Clubs 2006 ASID Designer Showhouse
Designer: Sally Trout
Photography: J. B. McCourtney

Pineapple House Interior Design, Inc. and Design Galleria

Atlanta Magazine Dream House 2006

Photography: John Umberger, Real Images

Pamela Hastings Interior Design Services

Boys' and Girls' Clubs 2002 ASID Designer Showhouse

Designer: Pamela Hastings, ASID

Photography: McCourtney Photographics

Kitchens

Liz At Home
Bellarmine University Women's Council Designers' Show House 2005
Designers: Katie Reese, Gabrielle Eurton, Jennifer Huber,
Kerry Nolan, Tiffany Wilson, Sharon Peckam, & Liz Wilson
Photography: Katie Woodring

Valerie Meyer Interior Design

Bellarmine University Women's Council Designers' Show House 2004
Designers: Valerie Meyer & Mike Cunningham
Photography: Katie Woodring

Wendy Holden & Associates
Mid-Atlantic Center for the Arts, Cape May 2006 Designer Show House
Designer: Wendy Holden
Photography: John Armich

Liz at Home

Bellarmine University Women's Council Designers' Show House 2006
Designers: Katie Reese, Gabrielle Eurton, Jennifer Huber,
Kerry Nolan, Tiffany Wilson, Sharon Peckam & Liz Wilson
Photography: Donna Borden

Patsy G. Interiors
Bellarmine University Women's Council Designers' Showhouse 2006
Designer: Patsy Grudzielanek
Photography: Donna Borden

Plum and Crimson Fine Interior Design

Vanguard/Albany Symphony Decorators' Showhouse 2007
Kitchen Installation: Builders Kitchen, Michelle Bucciero
Designers: Erika Gallagher & Denise Palumbo
Photography: Randall Perry

Cook's Design Studio

ASID Show House, St. Armands, FL 2003
Designers: Ron Cook, ASID & Margaret Cook, ASID
Photography: Dickenson Photography

T. M. Lewis Kitchens

Buffalo Jr. League Decorators' Show House 2007
Designer: Roseanne Driscoll, & T. M. Lewis
Photography: T. M. Lewis

Cook's Design Studio
ASID Show House, Sarasota, Florida 2004
Designers: Ron Cook, ASID & Margaret Cook, ASID
Photography: Greg Wilson Group

Cook's Design Studio

Cook's Design Studio

ASID Show House St. Armands, Florida 2006
Designers: Ron Cook, ASID & Margaret Cook, ASID
Photography: Gene Pollux

Cook's Design Studio
ASID Show House Harbor Dr. Sarasota, Florida 2005
Designers: Ron Cook, ASID & Margaret Cook, ASID
Photography: Greg Wilson Group

Magnolia Interiors

Mid-Atlantic Center for the Arts, Cape May 2006 Designer Showhouse
Designer: Susan Conroy
Photography: John Armich

Wellborn Forest
St. Jude Dream House Giveaway, Nashville, Tennessee
Designer: Franklin Kitchen Center
Photography: Schilling Photography

Pineapple House Interior Design, Inc. and Design Galleria

Atlanta Magazine Dream House 2006
Photography: John Umberger, Real Images

Teal Michel ASID, Interior Design

Symphony Guild ASID Showhouse, Charlotte, North Carolina
Designer: Teal Michel, Creative Design Solutions: Heather Littlewood Wojick
Photography: Ben Edmonson

Dining Rooms

Ethan Allen Home Interiors
Bellarmine University Women's Council Designers' Show House 2004
Photography: Katie Woodring

Domain Fabric & Interiors

Bellarmine University Women's Council Designers' Show House 2005
Designers: Christina Smith, Lauren Katz-Treese, & Jonathan Klunk
Photography: Katie Woodring

Pamela Hastings Interior Design
Boys' and Girls' Club 2007 ASID Designer Showhouse
Designer: Pamela Hastings, ASID
Photography: Mark Borosch

Custom Design Associates

Vanguard/Albany Symphony Decorators' Showhouse 2005
Designers: Mary Korzinski & Melissa Hatch
Decorative Painting: Elizabeth Rae Art Studios, Betsy Rae Mattice
Photography: Randall Perry

Custom Design Associates
Vanguard/Albany Symphony Decorators' Showhouse 2006
Designers: Mary Korzinski & Melissa Hatch
Photography: Randall Perry

Bebe Winkler Interior Design, Inc

Designers Fare 2003
Designers: Bebe Winkler & Michael Orsini
Photography: William P. Steele

Classic Interiors
Vanguard/Albany Symphony Decorators' Showhouse 2006
Designers: Lynn Ricci & Jessica Hartgraves
Photography: Randall Perry

Thomasville Home Furnishings

Vanguard/Albany Symphony Decorators' Showhouse 2007
Designer: Jeffery Ture
Photography: Randall Perry

Gomez
Kips Bay Showhouse 2007
Designer: Gomez
Photography: Nick Johnson

Kelley Interior Designs

Designer Show House, Easton, Maryland 2006
Designer: Kelley Proxmire
Photography: Angie Seckinger

Kelley Interior Designs
CFD Winter Show House, Annapolis, Maryland 2006
Designer: Kelley Proxmire
Photography: Angie Seckinger

Ethan Allen Furniture
Junior League of Buffalo Decorators' Show House 2007
Designers: Michael Michalski, Cindy Slomovitz, Lori Brennan, & Jillian McKee
Photography: © Michael Mandolfo

Dining
Al Fresco

Bacari Design Inc.
Baltimore Symphony Decorators' Showhouse 2007
Designer: Brenton Bacari
Photography: Angie Seckinger

Stephenson Interiors, LLC
Boys' and Girls' Club 2007 ASID Designer Showhouse
Designer: Harriet Stephenson, Allied ASID
Photography: Mark Borosch

Michele Hughes Design
Pasadena Showcase House of Design 2007
Designer: Michele Hughes Hayes, Allied Member ASID
Photography: Kathryn Russell Photography

Harmonious Living, LLC
Atlanta Magazine 2005
Designer: Tish Mills Design Group
Photography: Chris Little Photography

Moose Creek, Ltd.
Vanguard/Albany Symphony Designer Showhouse 2007
Designer: Patricia DeMento, & Stephen Momrow
Photography: Randall Perry

Mediterranean Villa Design Center

Boys' and Girls' Clubs 2006 ASID Designer Showhouse
Designer: Lisa Brecher, ASID
Photography by Lisa Brecher

Jessica Nixon Interior Design
Symphony Showhouse 2004
Designer: Jessica Nixon
Photography: Annile B. Rameriez

Bedrooms

Your Home
Bellarmine University Women's Council Designers' Show House 2004
Designers: Phillip Wheeler, & Jason Beck
Photography: Katie Woodring

Interior Marketplace
Bellarmine University Women's Council Designers' Show House 2006
Designer: Cay Cassady
Photography: Donna Borden

Amanda Moon Design

Bellarmine University Women's Council Designers' Show House 2005
Designer: Amanda Moon
Photography: Katie Woodring

Ethan Allen Home Interiors

Bellarmine University Women's Council Designers' Show House 2006
Designers: Kathy Snyder, Lauren Mills, Kay Shewanick,
Judy Keithley, Leslie Newton-Thompson, & Diane Hayter
Photography: Donna Borden

Burdorf's

Bellarmine University Women's Council Designers' Showhouse 2006
Designer: Suzanne Pruitt
Photography: Donna Borden

Gibraltar Homes

Boys' and Girls' Club 2007 ASID Designer Showhouse
Designers: Laura Strelser, ASID & Melissa Wollard, ASID
Photography: Mark Borosch

Kanes of Sarasota

Boys' and Girls' Club 2007 ASID Designer Showhouse
Designers: Betty DeArk, Allied ASID & Darcy Darcy, Allied ASID
Photography: Mark Borosch

Embellishments
Boys' and Girls' Club 2007 ASID Designer Showhouse
Designer: Cheri Pachter-Neary, Allied ASID
Photography: Mark Borosch

Provita Enterprises

Boys' and Girls' Club 2007 ASID Designer Showhouse
Designer: Ramina Azeem, Allied ASID
Photography: Mark Borosch

Accents & Design & S'Paschel Designs
Boys' and Girls' Club 2007 ASID Designer Showhouse
Designers: Patricia Lawrence, ASID IDS, & Carol Peschel, Allied ASID
Photography: Mark Borosch

Sterling Design Services
Boys' and Girls' Club 2007 ASID Designer Showhouse
Designer: Candy Gadd, Allied ASID
Photography: Mark Borosch

Blairhouse Interiors Group, Inc.
Vanguard/Albany Symphony Designer Showhouse 2005
Photography by Randall Perry

PMY Interiors

Vanguard/Albany Symphony Designer Showhouse 2006
Designer: Paula M. Yedynak
Photography: Randall Perry

Custom Design Associates

Vanguard/Albany Symphony Designer Showhouse 2006
Designers: Mary Korzinski & Melissa Hatch
Photography: Randall Perry

About Space

Vanguard/Albany Symphony Designer Showhouse 2007
Designers: Louise Westervelt, & Craig Taylor
Photography: Randall Perry

Beverly Taylor Design
ASID Designer Showhouse, Raleigh, North Carolina 2005
Designer: Beverly Taylor, ASID
Photography: Seth Tice-Lewis

Distinctive Interiors

Mid-Atlantic Center for the Arts, Cape May 2006 Designer Showhouse
Designer: Bernadette Kocis
Photography: John Armich

Yvonne Gregory Interiors, LLC
Charleston Symphony Design Show House, 2005
Designer: Yvonne Gregory, Allied Member ASID
Photography: Schultz Publications

J. Waddell Interiors

Bellarmine University Women's Council Designers' Show House 2004
Designers: Joan Waddell, CID, Allied ASID, Professional IDS & Carolyn Guetig
Photography: Katie Woodring

Kelley Interior Designs

Home & Design Magazine & DC Design Center Spring Design House, 2007
Designer: Kelley Proxmire
Photography: Angie Seckinger

Drake Design Associates
Kips Bay Showhouse 2007
Designer: Jamie Drake
Photography: Nick Johnson

Jed Johnson Associates
Kips Bay Showhouse 2007
Designer: Jed Johnson
Photography: Nick Johnson

Deborah R. Hill Interiors
Junior League of Buffalo Decorators' Show House 2007
Designer: Deborah Hill
Photography: © 2007 Michael Mandolfo

Mark Taylor Interiors

Junior League of Buffalo Decorators' Show House 2007
Designer: Mark Taylor
Photography: © 2007 Michael Mandolfo

Nancy Forare Cassidy Interior Design

Mid-Atlantic Center for the Arts, Cape May 2006 Designer Showhouse
Designer: Nancy Forare Cassidy
Photography: John Armich

Dragonfly Interiors, LLC
Mid-Atlantic Center for the Arts, Cape May 2006 Designer Showhouse
Designer: Jan Schmidt
Photography: John Armich

Fitz Interior Design, LLC

Mid-Atlantic Center for the Arts, Cape May 2006 Designer Showhouse
Designer: Tony Hawkins
Photography: John Armich

Cape May Linen Outlet
Mid-Atlantic Center for the Arts, Cape May 2006 Designer Showhouse
Designer: Nora Pascarella
Photography: John Armich

Stoess Manor and Claudia's @ Stoess
Bellarmine University Women's Council Designers' Show House 2005
Designers: Claudia Stoess & Leigh Stoess
Photography: Katie Woodring

Pedlar's Village Interior Design

Boys' and Girls' Clubs 2006 ASID Designer Showhouse
Designers: Gary Ficht & Susan Frick
Photography: Greg Wilson Photography

Moscato Interiors

Symphony Decorators' Showhouse, 2007
Designer: Maria Moscato
Photography: Alan Gilbert Photography

Rona Landman Inc.
International Designer Showhouse NYC 2005
Designer: Rona Landman
Photography: Peter Rymwid

Harmonious Living, LLC

Atlanta Magazine 2005
Designer: Tish Mills Design Group
Photography: Ken Rada Photography

Teal Michel ASID, Interior Design

Symphony Guild ASID Showhouse, Charlotte, NC
Designer: Teal Michel
Photography: Teal Michel, ASID

Custom Interiors and Jinx Inx. Interiors

Vanguard/Albany Symphony Designer Showhouse 2005
Designers: Karlene Cusick, & Jinx Van Steemberg
Photography: Randall Perry

Window Wear, Etc.

Vanguard/Albany Symphony Designer Showhouse 2005
Designer: Terry L. Kral
Photography: Randall Perry

Milieu Design Group

Christmas House 2006

Designer: Margaret Norcott
Photography: Burt Welleford

Children's
Bedrooms

Designer's Secrets

Mid-Atlantic Center for the Arts, Cape May 2006 Designer Showhouse

Designer: Elaine Finn
Photography: John Armich

Interior Image

Vanguard/Albany Symphony Designer Showhouse 2007
Designer: Sharon Askew
Photography: Randall Perry

Loulou's Whimsicals

Mid-Atlantic Center for the Arts, Cape May 2006 Designer Showhouse
Designer: LouLou Marshall
Photography: John Armich

CJ Designs

Vanguard/Albany Symphony Designer Showhouse 2005
Designers: Cheryl-Judge Decker, & Susan A. Munday
Mural: Rae Rau, PaintFx
Decorative Painting: Mary Beth Johnson, A.R.T.
Photography: Randall Perry

Lanes End Decorative Arts

Mansions in May Showhouse, Bernardsville, New Jersey, 2003
Designers: Patricia J. McWhorter, Ethan Allen Home Interiors, Designer: Dawn Mullins
Photography: Top Kay Photography

M Interiors

Designer Showhouse & Gardens 2006
Designer: Michelle G. Olson
Photography: Peter Gourniak

Bathrooms

Kimura Design
Bellarmine University Women's Council Designers' Show House 2005
Designer: Sandy Kimura
Photography: Katie Woodring

Creative Interiors

Bellarmine University Women's Council Designers' Show House 2005
Designer: Gay Lynn
Photography: Katie Woodring

Arts/Desire
Bellarmine University Women's Council Designers' Show House 2005
Designer: Natasha Pitcock
Photography: Katie Woodring

L&S Designs, LLC

Bellarmine University Women's Council Designers' Show House 2006
Designers: Stephanie Casenhiser & Leigh Anne Ferreri
Photography: Donna Borden

Michael E. Sams Interiors
Bellarmine University Women's Council Designers' Show House 2006
Designer: Michael Sams
Photography: Donna Borden

Palazzina
Bellarmine University Women's Council Designers' Showhouse 2006
Designers: Buff Fallott, ASID, KYCID, Sheeran King, & Janela James
Photography: Donna Borden

Burdorf's

Bellarmine University Women's Council Designers' Showhouse 2006
Designer: Suzanne Pruitt
Photography: Donna Borden

Tidmore-Henry Associates
Boys' and Girls' Club 2007 ASID Designer Showhouse
Designer: Tracey Ierulli, Allied, ASID
Photography: Mark Borosch

Robb & Stucky Interiors
Boys' and Girls' Club 2007 ASID Designer Showhouse
Designer: Greg Richardson, Allied ASID
Photography: Mark Borosch

Denise Maurer Interiors

Vanguard/Albany Symphony Designer Showhouse 2006
Designer: Denise Maurer
Decorative Painter: Elizabeth Rae Art Studios, Betsy Rae Mattice
Photography: Randall Perry

Tile Market
Boys' and Girls' Club 2007 ASID Designer Showhouse
Designer: Brigid Hewes, Allied ASID
Photography: Mark Borosch

Designed Interiors and Planning, Inc.
Boys' and Girls' Club 2007 ASID Designer Showhouse
Designer: Candis Scott, ASID
Photography: Mark Borosch

Natalie Howe Designs
Austin Women's Symphony League Show House 2007
Designer: Natalie Howe
Photography: Casey Dunn

Kimberly Petruska Designs

Society of the Arts Show House 2006
Designer: Kimberly Petruska
Decorative Artists: Carol Koenig Design Elements: Cindy Massa
Photography: Peter Gourniak

Mark Taylor Interiors
Junior League of Buffalo Decorators' Show House 2007
Designer: Mark Taylor
Photography: © 2007 Michael Mandolfo

East Coast Designs, LLC
& Shellter Fine Home Furnishings
Mid-Atlantic Center for the Arts, Cape May 2006 Designer Showhouse
Designer: Jill Traister
Photography: John Armich

Mural Mural on the Wall
Bellarmine University Women's Council
Designers' Show House 2004
Designers: Leigh Ann Ferreri & Cheryl Mahan
Photography: Katie Woodring

Rottger Construction, LLC
Junior League of Buffalo Decorators' Show House 2007
Designer: John Rottger
Photography: © 2007 Michael Mandolfo

Milieu Design Group

Christmas House 2006
Designer: Margaret Norcott
Photography: Burt Welleford

L. Marbury Designs
Bellarmine University Women's Council Designers' Show House 2004
Designers: Libby Marbury & Susan Lepping
Photography: Katie Woodring

L. Marbury Designs

Lanes End Decorative Arts
Mansions in May Showhouse 2006
Designer and Artist: Patricia J. McWhorter
Decorative Painter: Annette DeMetro
Interior Designer: Leigh Bollinger
Photography: John Martinelli

Special Purpose Rooms

Totten-McGuirl Fine Interiors
Mansion in May Showhouse 2006
Designers: William J. Totten & Linda Guy McGuirl
Photographer: Paul S. Bartholomew Photography, Inc.

Cherry House Furniture Galleries

Bellarmine University Women's Council Designers' Show House 2004
Designers: Natasha Pitcock & Grenda Black
Photography: Katie Woodring

Morris Dore Interiors

Bellarmine University Women's Council Designers' Show House 2004
Designers: Karen Morris & Tracee Dore Brown
Photography: Katie Woodring

Tassels

Bellarmine University Women's Council Designers' Show House 2005
Designers: Marsha Riggle & Kevin Coleman
Photography: Katie Woodring

Christine Brown
Interior Design, Inc.

2007 Boys' and Girls' Club
ASID Designer Showhouse
Designer: Christine Brown, ASID
Photography: Mark Borosch

Beth Boyce Design

Boys' and Girls' Club 2007 ASID Designer Showhouse
Designer: Beth Boyce, Allied, ASID
Photography: Mark Borosch

Robb & Stucky Design

Boys' and Girls' Club 2007 ASID Designer Showhouse
Designer: Joyce Hart, Allied ASID
Photography: Mark Borosch

Custom Design Associates
Vanguard/Albany Symphony Designers' Showhouse 2007
Designer: Mary Korzinski & Melissa Hatch
Photography: Randall Perry

Creative Storage

Buffalo Junior League Decorators' Show House 2007
Designer: Diana Auspurger
Photography: Sandi Kidman of Acorn Studios

The Home Stylist

2007 Junior League of Buffalo's
Decorators' Showhouse
Designer: Julie Dana
Photography: Stephen Smith

J. Hirsch Interior Design
Decorator Show House & Garden, 2006 Atlanta Georgia
Designer: Janie Hirsch, ASID, IFDA
Photography: Robert Thien, Inc.

Natalie Howe Designs

Austin Women's Symphony League Show House 2007
Designer: Natalie Howe
Photography: Casey Dunn

Van Galio & Fierle Design
Junior League of Buffalo Decorators' Show House 2007
Designers: Cathy VanGalio & Mimi Fierle
Photography: © 2007 Michael Mandolfo

Jessica Nixon Interior Design

Symphony Showhouse 2006

Designer: Jessica Nixon

Photography: Coles Hairston Photography

Tidmore-Henry & Associates

Boys and Girls Clubs 2006 ASID Designer Showhouse
Designers: William Tidmore & Robert Henry
Photography: Greg Wilson Group

Stanton Home Furnishings

Atlanta Symphony Associates Decorators' Showhouse and Gardens, 2007
Designer: Jimmy Stanton
Photography: Mali Azima

Stanton Home Furnishings

Atlanta Symphony Associates Decorators' Showhouse and Gardens, 2007
Designer: Jimmy Stanton
Photography: Mali Azima

Plumberry Designs, Inc.
Mansions in May Designer Showhouse 2006
Designer: Richard Barr
Photography: Tom Sperduto

Whitney Design & Associates

Boys' and Girls' Clubs 2006 ASID Designer Showhouse
Designer: Thomas G. Stanley ASID
Photography: Pollux Photography & Digital Imaging

Liz At Home

Bellarmine University Women's Council Designers' Show House 2004
Designers: Liz Wilson, Gabrielle Everton, Jennifer Huber, Tara Shackelford,
Katie Reese, Tiffany Wilson, Sharen Peckham, Kelly Piepenhoff, & Tammy Randell
Photography: Katie Woodring

Vital Design LTD
Kips Bay Show House, New York 2007
Designer: Cheryl Terrace
Photography: Richard Cadan

Michele Hughes Design

Pasadena Showcase House of Design 2007
Designer: Michele Hughes Hayes, Allied Member ASID
Photography: Kathryn Russell Photography

Harmonious Living, LLC
Children's Alliance Theater Christmas House 2004
Designer: Tish Mills Design Group
Photography: Ken Rada Photography

Design!

If you're interested in architecture, landscaping, graphic design, fashion or any other form of the visual arts, we've got hundreds of inspiring books. Schiffer Publishing, Ltd. has worked hard to cultivate a broad backlist of titles, each packed to the endpages with visual stimulation. You simply get more pictures per page, more pages per book, and better color reproduction and book production quality than most publishing houses are willing to invest in. Our sumptuous books are worth every penny, because we've spent millions making sure that you find inspiring color and detail every time you open the covers.

Be sure to get our print catalogs with over 3,200 titles by calling U.S. 610-593-1777, or visit our website at:
www.schifferbooks.com.
Most importantly, be sure to support your local book dealers when it is time to expand your library.

Showhouses

The following websites and text help provide more illumination about many of the showhouses and charitable organizations that participated in the production of this book.

Architectural Digest Home Design Show
Website: archdigesthomeshow.com

The Architectural Digest Home Design Show attracted an attendance of more than 26,000 consumers and designers over four event-filled days. Visitors shopped for home design products, including art, attended designer seminars and keynote speeches, participated in complimentary design consultations and experienced live cooking demonstrations and book signings.

ASID Florida West Chapter Designer Show House
Website: asidfloridawestcoast.com

Over the past 10 years ASID has contributed in excess of $125,000 to The Boys' and Girls' Club and its generosity has helped increase public awareness of the needs of youth in our community. More than one million dollars have been generated for the clubs in Manatee and Sarasota counties in in-kind donations and scholarships as a result of the Showhouse event and the ongoing marketing exposure.

Atlanta Magazine Dream House
Website:charityguild.org

Atlanta Magazine Dream Home partnered with the Country Club of the South Charity Guild in 2005. The guild is a non-profit volunteer organization dedicated to improving the Atlanta community by raising funds for local charities. In the fifteen years since the group began, the Country Club of the South Charity Guild has donated over $2 million to local charities.

Atlanta Symphony Decorators Show House and Gardens
Websites: atlantasymphony.org & decorator-showhouse.org

Proceeds from this event benefit the Atlanta Symphony Orchestra's Learning Community, which is the largest provider of music education in the southeast, annually reaching more than 50,000 young people through music training programs and educational concerts.

Women's Symphony League of Austin
Website: austinsymphony.org/get_involved/wsl/

Bellarmine University Women's Council Designers' Show
Website: bellarmine.edu/alumni/womenscouncil/

Since 1974 the Bellamine University Women's Council has presented a historic Designer's Show House. Each year an all-volunteer organization has raised funds for the Student Financial Aid Fund with proceeds amounting to over $1.5 million.

Beverly Hills Garden & Design Showcase
Website: beverlyhills.org

Buffalo Junior League Decorators' Show House
Website: jlbuffalo.com

Since 1981 The Junior League of Buffalo has collaborated with the Buffalo News every two years on show houses that have raised over $2.5 million for projects benefiting the western New York community while rehabilitating dilapidated buildings.

Center For Family Development Show House
Website: discover-annapolis.com/hollytrollr/dichouse

Charleston Symphony Design Showhouse
Website: csonlinc.org

This year's Showhouse was built in 1853 by Sara Smith as one of four row houses in what is known as Bee's Row. The house was used as a dry goods store during the Civil War, survived the 1885 earthquake, and was used as a convent in the later portion of the twentieth century.

Children's Alliance Theatre Show House
Website: alliancechristmashouse.org

The Christmas House 2006 is a celebration of children, beautiful homes, and the spirit of Christmas. All proceeds go to support the Alliance Children's Theatre, which is recognized nationally for its presentation of classical and original literature adapted into plays for children.

Harrisburg Symphony Showhouse
Website: harrisburgsymphony.org

Kips Bay Show House
Website: kipsbay.org/showhouse.html

Mansion in May
Website: wammh.org

This celebrated biennial designer Showhouse fundraiser of the Women's Association of Morristown Memorial Hospital, an all volunteer group. Since it began in 1974, Mansion in May has raised $3.7 million for the hospital.

Cape May Designer Show House
Website: capemaymac.com

The Mid-Atlantic Center for the Arts is a non-profit organization dedicated to the preservation and interpretation of Cape May, New Jersey's heritage and fostering the performing arts.

National Symphony Orchestra Show House
Website: kennedy-center.org/showhouse.

Pasadena Showcase House of the Designs
Website: pasadenashowcasee.org

Since 1989, the Pasadena Showcase House for the Arts has awarded approximately $2 million in monetary grants to non-profit organizations and schools in addition to major gifts to the Los Angeles Philharmonic. Grants are awarded in support of music-oriented programs. They have enabled the purchase of musical instruments, music therapy programs for abused and neglected children and music education in local schools and nonprofit organizations as well as the underwriting of musical concerts within the greater Los Angeles area.

Society of the Arts Showhouse
Website: sotashowhouse.org

Baltimore Symphony Decorator Show House
Website: Baltimoresymphony.org

St. Jude Dream House Giveaway benefiting the St. Jude Cancer Research Hospitla for Children
Website: dreamhouse@stjude.org

Vanguard/Albany Symphony Show House
Website: albanysymphony.com

Vanguard is an all-volunteer organization, which exists to support the Albany Symphony Orchestra. Its chief fund-raiser is its annual Designer Showhouse, which was held in 2007 for the twenty-seventh time.

Washington, D.C., Design Center
Website: www.mmart.com/dcdesigncenter

In its seventeenth iteration, Design House has developed as the preeminent showcase for local design talent to showcase the luxury products available exclusively through Washington Design Center showrooms.

Designers

Following is a list of decorators and design firms whose work is represented in this book.

About Space
Greenfield Center, NY
518-893-2044
about-space.com

ArtfulLiving
Madison, TN
812-265-6262
artfulliving.info

Arts/Desire
Louisville, KY
502-493-2229

Amanda Moon Design
Louisville, KY
502-589-2738

Beverly Taylor Design
Raleigh, NC
919-847-4717
Beverly@beverlyTaylorDesign.com

Brenton Bacari
Washington, DC
202-518-0110
bacaridesign.com

Baker-Wooley Interiors
Rensselaerville, NY 12147
518-797-9303
bakerwooleyinteriors.com

Healing Barsanti, Inc.
Patricia Healing & Daniel Barsanti
Westport, CT
203-226-5105
daniel@healingbasanti.com

Bebe Winkler Interior Design, Inc.
New York, NY
212-308-5674

Bittners, LLC
Louisville, KY
502-584-6349

Blairhouse Interiors Group, Inc.
Newtonville, NY 12128
518-786-7800
blairhouseinteriors.com

The Blue Nest
Louisville, KY
502-394-9200

Beth Boyce Designs
Sarasota, FL
941-358-7737

Burdorf's
Louisville, KY
502-719-9700

Builder's Kitchen
Albany, NY
518-438-0323
builderskitchen.com

Mario Buatta, Inc.
New York, NY
212-988-6811
mariobuatta@aol.com

Calico Corners
Louisville, KY
502-327-0944

Carl Harz Furniture
Elmer, NJ
856-358-7241

Nancy Forare Cassidy
Vincentown, NJ
609-238-4146

Cape May Linen Outlet
West Cape May, NJ
609-884-3630
capemaylinen.com

Cherry House Furniture Galleries
LaGrange, KY
502-425-7107

Chochkeys
Buffalo, NY
716-882-0052
chochkeys@adelphia.net

CJ Designs
Mechanicsville, NY
518-469-3831
deckercj22@cs.com

Christine Brown Interior Designers
Inc., ASID
Sarasota, FL
941-921-6256

Christopher Gaona Interiors, Inc.
Los Angeles, CA
213-749-3324
christophergaona.com

Classic Interiors
Clifton Park, NY
518-383-2678
classicinteriors.com

CMH Design
Rotterdam, NY
518-280-2104
chmdesign@nycap.rr.com

Cook's Design Studio
Sarasota, FL
941-366-6112

Creative Interiors by Gay Lynn
Crestwood, KY
502-468-6835

Creative Storage
Buffalo, NY
morestorage.com
716-871-1474

Custom Design Associates
Clifton Park, NY
518-899-3182

Deborah Hill Interiors
Buffalo, NY
716-870-6803

Denise Maurer Interiors
Troy, NY
518-273-2133
denisemaurer@aol.com

Designed Interiors and Planning, Inc.
Bradenton, FL
941-538-0027

Designer's Secrets
Cincinnati, OH
513-752-1023

Details Interiors
Louisville, KY
502-253-0092

Distinctive Interiors
Cape May, NJ
609-884-6483

Domain Fabric & Interiors
Louisville, KY
502-893-3334

Dragonfly Interiors, LLC
Cape May, NJ
609-884-3200

Drake Design Associates
New York, NY
212.754.3099
jamiedrake@drakedesignassociates.com

East Coast Designs, LLC
& Shellter Fine Home Furnishings
Ocean City, NJ
609-410-8833

Embellishments
Sarasota, FL
941-331-8025

Nathan Egan Interiors
New York NY
212.414.1313
wnathan@nathanegan.com
cegan@nathanegan.com

Elizabeth Rae Art Studios
Delmar, NY 12054
518-439-2300
elizabethraeart.zoomshare.com

Eric Schmidt Interiors
New York, NY
212-288-3431
ericschmidtinteriors.com

Ethan Allen Furniture
Amhearst, NY
716- 839-4484

Ethan Allen Home Interiors
Louisville, KY
502-426-4594

Eve Robinson Associates, Inc.
New York, NY
212-595-0661
eve@everobinson.net

Experience and Creative Design,
Ltd.
Schenectady, NY
experienceandcreativedesign.com
518-374-6885

Fitz Interior Design, LLC
Bloomfield, NY
607-538-1753

Gary Stewart Interiors
Louisville, KY
502-899-1537

Gibraltar Homes
Sarasota, FL
941-366-1442

Gomez
New York, NY 10021
212.288.6856

Gryphon Interiors, Inc.
Louisville, KY
502-893-7900

Hubbuch & Company
Louisville, KY
502-583-2713
hubbuch.com

The Home Stylist
East Aurora, NY
716-912-1581,
Julie@thehomestylist.com

Hudson River Fine Interiors
Loudonville, NY
518-463-3969
HudsonRiverFineInteriors.com

Interior Image
S. Bethlehem, NY
518-767-2206
interiorimage.com

Interior Marketplace
Louisville, KY
502-894-9955
interiormp.com

Interiors by Herbal Accents
Anchorage, KY
502-489-5511

The Noel Jeffery Design Group,
Inc.
New York, NY 10021
212.935.7775
noelj@noeljeffery.com

Jed Johnson Associates
New York, NY
212.707.8989
tom@jedjohnson.com

Mary Beth Johnson, A.R.T.
Troy, NY
279-4989
marybethjohnson.com

John Rottger Construction, LLC
Buffalo, NY
716-832-0023

J Hirsch Interior Design
Cummings, GA
770-781-2868
jhirschinteriors.com

Jinx Inx. Interiors
Loudonville, NY
518-462-2026
jinx1953@msn.com

J Waddell Interiors, LLC
Louisville, KY
502-897-6566
JwaddellInteriors@aol.com

khl Studio
914-941-1735
khlstudio@verizon.net

Kanes of Sarasota
Sarasota, FL
941-924-1271

Karlene Cusick Custom Interiors
Loudonville, NY
518-463-3441
karlenejoe@aol.com

Kelley Interior Designs
Bethesda, MD
301-320-2109
Kelley.kelleyIDS@comcast.net

Kenneth/Davis, Architecture and
Interior Design
Pompton Plains, NJ
973-248-0870

Kimberly Petruska Designs
Emmaus, PA
610-966-5836
kepetruska@enter.net

Kimura Design
Louisville, KY
502-254-9486

Carol Koenig Interior Designer-
Furnishings
Allentown, PA 18014
610-439-3882

Las Casitas Architecture and Planning
Sarasota, FL
941-922-1562

Lancaster Humma White Studios
Sarasota, FL
941-365-2342
lancasterhummawhite.com

La Bella Casa Designs, LLC
Red Bank, NJ
732-530-1632

Lands End Decorative Arts
Oak Ridge, NJ
973-697-4620
landsenddecorativearts.com

Lewis Interiors
Louisville, KY
502-425-7849

L. Marbury Designs
Prospect, KY
502-228-9258

Nora Logan
Rensselaerville, NY
518-797-3243
nlogan522@aol.com

Loulou's Whimsicals
Unionville, PA
484-680-4487
LouLou'swhimsicals.com

Liz At Home
New Albany, IN
812-949-9094

L&S Designs, LLC
Louisville, KY
502-767-2647

Magnolia Interiors
Ocean City, NJ
609-391-7772

Design Elements
Allentown, PA 18104
610-437-3303

Mediterranean Villa Design Center
Sarasota, FL
941-366-2869

Mary Beth Johnson
Troy, NY
518-279-4989
MaryBethJohnson.com

Michael Donnelly Interiors
Buffalo, NY
716- 308-6520

Michele Hughes Designs
Pasadena, CA
626-578-9700
michelehughesdesign.com

Micheline LaBerge
Sarasota, FL
941-924-1778
michelineasid.com

Michael E. Sams Interiors
Corydon, IN
812-738-6020

Michelle Olsen
Allentown, PA
610-653-6667

Morris Dore Interiors
Louisville, KY
502-895-0110

Moose Creek Ltd.
Albany, NY
518-869-0049
moosecreekltd.com

Mural Mural on the Wall
Louisville, KY
502-326-9105

Norwalk – The Furniture Idea
North Wales, PA
215-646-2000

Natalie Howe Designs
Austin, TX
512-382-0548
Natalie@nataliehowedesign.com

Nora Logan Studios
Rensselaerville, NY
518-797-3243

PaintFx
Rae Rau
Guilderland, NY 12084
518-598-8916

Palazzina
Louisville, KY
502-897-7870

Pamela Hastings, ASID
Sarasota, FL
941-953-9703
FL ID 1950

Patsy G. Interiors
Louisville, KY
502-326-5005

Patricia Lawrence, ASID, IDS
Bradenton, FL
941-755-5216

Pedlar's Village Interior Design
Sarasota, FL
941-955-5726
pedlarsvillage.com

Plum & Crimson Fine Interior
Design
Clifton Park, NY
518-373-2009
plumandcrimson.com

PMY Interiors
Niskayuna, NY
518-366-8135
518-608-5554

Plumberry Designs, Inc.
Florsham Park, NJ
973-966-1950
plumberry.net

Protiva Enterprises
Sarasota, FL
941-926-7209

Quaker Country Home
Orchard Park, NY
667-1541
quakercounrtyhome.com

Remarkable Interiors
Prospect, KY
502-228-8288
remarkableinteriors.com

Robb & Stuckey Interiors
Sarasota, FL
941-922-2274

Rona Langman,
New York, NY
212-421-1566

Roseanne Driscoll Interior Design
716-491-3182

Sally Trout Interiors
Sarasota, FL
941-953-4418

Stephen Miller Seigel Architects
New York, NY
212.832.5400

S'Peschel Designs
Longboat Key, FL
941-383-0538

Stephenson Interiors, LLC
Osprey, FL
941-966-2410

Sterling Design Services
Sarasota, FL
941-232-8155

Sutton's Marketplace
Queensbury, NY
518-798-0133
suttonsmarketplace.com

Stanton Home Furnishings
Atlanta, GA
404-586-9000

SA Home Designer
San Antonio, TX
210-520-3100

Stoess Manor and Claudia's @
Stoess
Crestwood, KY
502-241-8494

The Replogle House Interiors
Mechanicsburg, PA
717-691-1185
reploglehouse interiors.com

Tassels
Louisville, KY
502-245-7887

Mark Taylor Interiors
Buffalo, NY
716-881-0120
716-830-8984

Teal Michel, ASID Interior Design
Charlotte, NC
704-554-7035
tealmichelasid.com

The Home Stylist
East Aurora, NY
716-912-1581
thehomestylist.com

Thomasville Home Furnishings
Colonie, NY
518-435-2333
thomasville-albany.com

Tidmore-Henry & Associates
Sarasota, FL
941-955-4427
941-954-4454

Totten-McGuirl Fine Interiors
Basking Ridge, NJ
908-580-9572
totten-mcguirl.com

T.M. Lewis Kitchens
Londonville, NY
716-812-8619

Valerie Meyer Interior Designs
Louisville, KY
502-635-0147

Van Galio & Fierle Design
Buffalo, NY
716-687-4833

Vidal Design
New York, NY
212-799-1540
vitaldesign.ltd.com

Wendy Holden & Associates
Moorestown, NJ
856-234-1130

Whitney Design & Associates
Sarasota, FL
941-358-6700

Whitney Stewart Interior Design
Washington, DC
202-537-0050

Window Wear, Etc.
Schenectady, NY
518-355-0063
WindowWearEtc.com

Your Home
Jeffersonville, IN
812-284-1739

Yvonne Gregory Interiors, LLC
Mt. Pleasant, SC
843-881-6291

Photographers

The following photographers have work featured in this book.

Acorn Studios
Sandra Kieman
East Amherst, NY 14051
716-639-1306

John Armich Photography
armich@johnarmich.com

Mali Azima
Atlanta, GA
404-510-2271
maliazima.com

Paul S. Bartholomew Photography, Inc.
paul@pbsphoto.com

Mark Borosch Photography
markborosch.com
813-781-9368
Tampa Bay, FL

Richard Cadan
richardcadan.com

Coles Hairston Photography
Austin, TX
512-416-6060
coles@coleshairston.com

Kinsley Dey Photography
deyphoto.com

Seth Tice-Lewis Photography
wwwsethticelewis.com

Casey Dunn Photography
caseydunn.net
512-413-6846
Austin, TX

James Dean
JamesDeanPhoto.com

Dickenson Photography
Sarasota, FL 34236
941-955-9555

Ben Edmonson
Blackdogimages, LLC
704-376-2117

Phillip Ennis
phillipennis.com

Alan Gilbert Photography
Baltimore, MD 21211
Peter Gourniak
New York, N.Y.

Nick Johnson Photography
New York, NY
917-544-2264

Kathryn Russell Photography
South Pasadena, CA
626.404.1523
kathrynrussell.com

Chris Little Photography
Atlanta, GA
770-560-5551
chrislittlephotography.com

J. B. McCourtney
Sarasota, FL 34231
941-921-9151
941-346-0913

Michael Mandolfo Photography
michaelmandolfo.com

John Martinelli
Moorestown, NJ
johnmartinelliphotography.com

Andrea Mittica
AndreaMittica.com

John Paul
Louisville, KY
502-637-1957

Randall Perry
Schaghticoke, NY 12154
518-664-5122

Gene Pollux Photography
Sarasota, FL 34236
941-366-3456

Ken Rada Photography
Hoschton, GA 30548

Annile B. Rameriez
Austin, TX 78756

Lauren Rubenstein Photography
LARphotography.com
404-932-2815

Peter Rymwid
PeterRymwid.com

Walt Roycraft Photography
roycraftart.com
859-887-1891

Schultz Publications
Julie Schultz
Mt. Pleasant, SC
jeschultz@gmail.com

Angie Seckinger Photography
Potomac, MD
301-983-9846
angieseckinger.com

Shilling Photography
Dave Schilling
schillingphoto.com

Stephen Smith
Iron Images
ironimagesonline.com

Tom Sperduto
Edison. NJ
tomsperduto.com

William P. Steele
New York, NY
212-751-8282

Walter Smalling, Jr.
wasmalling.aol.com
202-234-2438

Top Kat Photography
Philadelphia, PA
215-235-6012

Robert Thien, Inc.
RobertThien.com
404-486-9813

John Umberger Photography
Real Images
Atlanta, GA
678-290-7800

The Washington Design Center
Washington, DC 20024
dcdesigncenter.com

Greg Wilson Photography
Sarasota, FL 34277
greg@gregwilsonphoto.com

Burt Wellford Photography
404-245-3670

Katie Woodring, Photography, LLC
Louisville, KY
katiewoodring.com

Designer Showcase: Interior Design at its Best.

Melissa Cardona & Nathaniel Wolfgang-Price.

In the past ten years, antique textiles, especially those from France, have become very popular for interior decoration. In her easy-to-read style, the author gives a basic history of French textiles from the Middle Ages to Art Déco. 416 beautiful color photographs demonstrate traditional and contemporary uses for tapestries, cottons, linens, laces, embroidery, needlepoint, and trims. Suggestions are given for their use in contemporary interior and home décor. Answers to frequently asked questions are very helpful to the novice and connoisseur alike. The clearly stated text explains how to recognize these fabrics in the marketplace and what to look for when purchasing them. A range of values for the examples shown reflects the current antiques market.

This is a book for the general public as well as for designers. Readers will gain the confidence to add a creative touch or note of elegance to their decorations and designs with antique textiles.

Size: 8 1/2" x 11" • 400 color photos • 256 pp.
ISBN: 0-7643-2398-9 • hard cover • $44.95

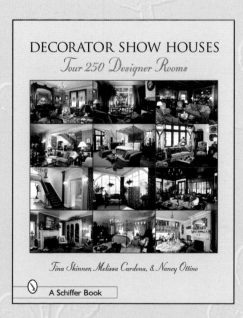

Decorator Show Houses: Tour 250 Designer Rooms.

Tina Skinner, Melissa Cardona, & Nancy Ottino.

Welcome to the Ultimate Decorator Event! For the price of admission to one show house and a modest luncheon, you'll get to tour 50 different show houses and over 250 spectacular rooms, where designers have pulled out all the stops to showcase their very best. Some of the most extraordinary work in interior design today is presented in 513 stunning color photographs. You'll see rooms saturated in glorious paint, windows dressed in the finest draperies, surfaces transformed with faux finishes, and furniture swathed in luxurious fabrics. Beginning the tour in foyers and hallways that leave lasting first impressions, you'll continue through glorious living rooms and family rooms that you'll never want to leave. Make your way through amazing libraries and home offices, dining rooms, kitchens, sunrooms, bedrooms, and bathrooms. You'll also get a chance to see innovative design ideas for media rooms, wine cellars, loft spaces, and bonus rooms. In this book you will find breathtaking and exciting designs that will inspire and amaze you, in addition to a list of extraordinary interior designers and annual show house events.

Size: 8 1/2" x 11" • 513 color photos • 224 pp. • hard cover
• ISBN: 0-7643-2051-3 • $44.95

Home Theaters and Electronic Houses. CEDIA & Tina Skinner. A colorful tour of sound-proofed, silver-screened retreats fit for movie stars, Starship commanders, and sultans. Visit amazing home theaters and high-tech homes, where room-by-room sensors and touch-pad controls put lighting, sound, temperature, and security at your command. Watch screens descend or ascend from unexpected hiding places, projectors appear, and windows disappear in James-Bond like mechanical transitions. And enjoy flat-screen and plasma entertainments in the most unexpected of places -- shower stalls, pool rooms, home sports bars, and more, tucked into basements, spare bedrooms, playrooms, garages, and even attics.

Size: 11" x 8 1/2" • 230+ color pictures •
176 pp. • ISBN: 0-7643-1957-4 • hard cover • $44.95

Home Office, Library, and Den Design. Tina Skinner. Visit more than 200 private offices, dens, and libraries. If you are looking for design inspiration, this book is packed with ideas for floor layouts, paneling and shelving systems, storage systems, and color schemes.

Size: 8 1/2" x 11" • 242 color photos • Resource Guide •
144 pp. • ISBN: 0-7643-1842-X • soft cover • $24.95

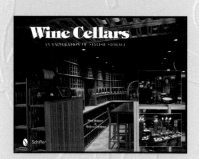

Wine Cellars: An Exploration of Stylish Storage. Tina Skinner & Melissa Cardona. This thorough and inspiring book provides a vicarious tour of the best in wine bottle storage. Visit more than 100 absolutely stunning, private wine cellars in over 200 beautiful color photographs. Peruse racking systems, tasting tables, and artful touches, created by leading wine cellar designers, including Paul Wyatt, Kathleen Valentini, Gary LaRose, and Doug Smith. Additionally, this is a guidebook to wine cellars in some of the world's most renowned hotels and restaurants.

Size: 11" x 8 1/2" • 200+ color photos •
160 pp. • ISBN: 0-7643-1965-5 • hard cover • $49.95

Designs for Restaurants & Bars: Inspiration from Hundreds of International Hotels. Tina Skinner. Tour more than 200 eating establishments worldwide, designed by David Rockwell, Ian Schrager, Robert DiLeonardo, Adam Tihany, Karl Lagerfeld, Pierre Court, Patrick Jouin, Philippe Starck, and more.

Size: 8 1/2" x 11" • 262 color photos • Resource Guide •
176 pp. • ISBN: 0-7643-1752-0 • hard cover • $39.95

Old World Kitchens and Bathrooms: A Design Guide. Melissa Cardona. Captures the textures, design, colors, and craftsmanship that evoke European ideals of a bygone era. Explore kitchens and baths rich in the fine details that characterize Provencal, Tuscan, and English country designs.

Size: 8 1/2" x 11" • 165 color photos • 112 pp. • soft cover • ISBN: 0-7643-2078-5 • $19.95

Traditional Style Kitchens: Modern Designs Inspired by the Past. Melissa Cardona. Early American, Colonial, Victorian, Shaker, and Arts & Crafts, in addition to Traditional Country and Farmhouse kitchens are shown in over 150 gorgeous color photos.

Size: 8 1/2" x 11" • 150+ color photos • 112 pp. • soft cover • ISBN: 0-7643-2285-0 • $19.95

Contemporary Kitchens: A Style Guide. Melissa Cardona. Hundreds of contemporary kitchens demonstrate sleek space-age designs, minimalist masterpieces, and traditional kitchens with a modern flair. Actual projects from top designers and cabinetry manufacturers will keep homeowners, architects, and designers turning the pages enthusiastically.

Size: 8 1/2" x 11" • 250+ color photos • 128 pp. • ISBN: 0-7643-2399-7 • soft cover • $24.95

The Window Treatment Workbook. Kristen Fitch. Over 600 artful watercolor renderings of window treatments combined with a CD of all the images make this the most useful, practical book available. Professional decorators and homeowners alike will love it.

Size: 8 1/2" x 11" • 600+ watercolor paintings • 96 pp. • 2 CD Roms • ISBN: 0-7643-2184-6 • $24.95